THESE
MEANINGFUL
MOMENTS *belong to:*

_____

_____

52 Meaningful Moments

a journal for finding joy & purpose,
right where you are

Anne McOmber

A Simplicity Avenue Project // SimplicityAvenue.com

Simplicity Avenue Media LLC
5526 West 13400 South #350, Herriman, UT 84065
www.SimplicityAvenue.com

Watercolor art by Iuliia Mironova
Cover and interior design by Anne McOmber

ISBN 978-0-692-18624-4
First edition, October 2018

Printed in the United States

for Matt, Shadyn, and Naomi

I love that our moments aren't only meaningful,

but happy, silly, and everything in between...

& that they're lived together.

CO NTE NTS

table of

moments of

welcome
seeker

There are moments in life that are undeniably... well, meaningful. They're moments that are held close to your heart - always to be remembered, cherished, and appreciated. But what about everything in between?

What about all the moments that aren't necessarily life-changing or precious, tender or special but just the ordinary moments that make up our days, months and years? **Is it even possible to live a happy, meaningful life right where you are?**

Much more than a journal, this book is a journey. And it begins with an open heart, fresh eyes, and the courage to move forward, one small step at a time. In short, it begins the second you put pen to paper.

To be perfectly honest, it's a journey not everyone is willing to take. In some way or another we all want to feel joy and purpose in our lives. But this adventure of actually claiming them is only made by the seekers... like you. The ones who are willing to dig deep and set out on a treasure hunt that's just as much about creating as it is about uncovering.

I don't know your struggles or strengths, your hopes or heartbreaks. I don't have a detailed view of where you're headed or the paths you've already followed. But I do know that - whether you believe it or not - you have a brave, beautiful life to live.

SO TURN THE PAGE, SEEKER,
AND BEGIN.

You can sit down for an epic writing session and take on a full section at a time or thoughtfully search for each meaningful moment weekly for a full year. Either way, it's time to see your life just as it is and uncover what's already there. Because the truth is your life's already full of meaningful moments. It's just a matter of discovering them.

love, Anne

IT'S TIME

TO SEE YOUR LIFE

JUST AS IT IS

& discover the goodness

THAT'S ALREADY

THERE.

for your journey

Meaningful moment seeker... it's a title I lovingly placed next to my name and on my heart before this book was even a spark of an idea. I smile at the idea of sharing it.

So I wrote a manifesto to make it official, then made it beautiful enough for your wall or refrigerator. I created some encouragement cards too for when the meaningful moments feel harder to find. You can head over to 52meaningfulmoments.com for your digital copy of both. Consider them a thank you gift and a *"welcome to the meaningful moment seeker family!"* wrapped up in one.

Wherever you are in your journey, the fact that you're holding this book and filling its pages means more to me than you know.

CONNECTION

moments of

Who in your life is experiencing success, excitement, or joy right now? Who can you be happy for?

Use this page to go beyond yourself and celebrate. Cheer for them. Spread light!

spread
light

How did someone change your day for the better?

An act of unexpected kindness? A friendly conversation with a stranger? Something that made you laugh 'til your mouth hurt?

nothing changes the day like a smile

If love - real, true, unconditional love -
could be bottled up in a single memory,
what memory would that be?

love
always

Who makes your life happy?

"No matter what I'm doing, being with _____ is better than doing the best thing in the world alone."

Make a list of the feelings they bring into your heart and soul.

live
from the
heart

moments of *GRATITUDE*

List the compliments people give you most often.

Soak in these words. Let them lift you.

_____

_____

_____

_____

_____

_____

_____

_____

_____

_____

_____

_____

_____

_____

_____

_____

_____

_____

_____   embrace

_____   the goodness

_____   others see

_____   in you

_____

_____

_____

_____

_____

_____

_____

What was the best part of today?

What piece of goodness from the last 24 hours is worth savoring?

When you can't be grateful for everything...

...be grateful for something.

When has someone come to your rescue?

Write about the experience from a perspective of gratitude, rather than guilt. Choose to let love in.

let
love in

What do you treasure?

*A hobby, traditions, talents, loved ones, notes
or trinkets that hold a piece of your heart?*

**Fill up every inch of these pages,
margins and all.**

*Life becomes
full of all kinds
of treasures...*

...once you start
looking for them.

moments of CREATIVITY

What did you create this week?

*A friendship, a clean or beautified space,
a new skill, a different perspective, a
delicious meal... Choose to look past
the flaws and see the beauty.*

*choose to
see the
beauty*

What is one thing you'd want to accomplish if you had no limits?

_____

_____

_____

_____

_____

_____

_____

_____

_____

_____

_____

_____

_____

_____

_____

_____

_____

_____

_____

_____

_____

_____

_____

_____

_____

_____

_____

_____

_____

_____

_____

_____

_____

_____

ps:
your potential is limitless

What have you grown from a tiny seed of inspiration?

Something you took from an idea to finished even though it could have easily been lost in the distractions and noise of life?

_____

_____

_____

_____

_____

_____

_____

_____

_____

_____

_____

What if you hadn't made it happen?

What goodness has come from bringing
that spark of an idea to life?

be inspired
to inspire

Write about a time you
created something for the
joy and fulfillment of creating.

No comparison, no perfectionism.
Just you being you.

_do more
than just
exist_

moments of POSITIVITY

What are you excited for today?
This week? This month?

decide today
will be
amazing

Write about a time when the outcome was so much better than you expected it would be.

Trust that the goodness is there...

...then get to work
looking for it.

What keeps getting between you and your happiness?

"If only _____ , then I'd be happy."

happiness is always within reach

_____

_____

_____

_____

_____

_____

_____

_____

_____

_____

_____

_____

_____

_____

_____

_____

*Now turn the page and leave
everything on these pages behind.*

16

What have you lost?

*A loved one, your health,
a job, a relationship?*

_____

_____

_____

_____

_____

_____

_____

_____

*you are
never alone* _____

_____

_____

List 3 unexpected gifts that came with your loss.

Maybe a better path you would never have found otherwise or an inner strength you would never have uncovered?

_____

_____

_____

_____

_____

_____

_____

_____

_____

_____

_____

CO
MPA
moments of
SSI
ON

How could your experience and perspective *(like what you wrote on pages 50-51)* **lift someone else?**

shine from
the heart

When have you brought happiness
to someone else as if your own
happiness depended on it?

grow
your
happiness...

...by giving it away.

List 5 qualities or talents that come effortlessly to you.

How could you use these gifts to brighten someone's day?

_____

_____

_____

_____

_____

_____

_____

_____

_____

_____

_____

_____

Be the
light...

...you
were meant
to be.

What did you give this week?

Love, a smile, a hot meal, service, encouragement, a hug, a compliment, a phone call, forgiveness...

spread
goodness

PRESENCE

moments of

When was the last time you listened to the rain? Or stared out the window instead of your phone?

Take a break from multi-tasking and spend the day really living in the moment. **Write about your experience here.**

_____

_____

_____

_____

_____

_____

_____

_____

_____

_____

_____

live life
through breaths,
not clicks

Deep breath in. Deep breath out. For the next 3 minutes write whatever comes to mind.

See the words on this page without judgement.

be here
now

List 10 simple pleasures that bring you comfort and happiness.

A special treat, hot shower, favorite song... Pick one to savor this week.

_____

_____

_____

_____

_____

_____

_____

_____

_____

_____

_____

_____

savor
the simple
things

Write about living a regret-free moment.

"I'm glad I took the time today to..."

this
moment
matters

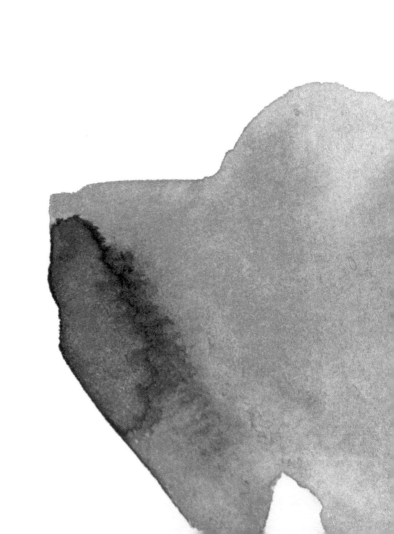

moments of REFLECTION

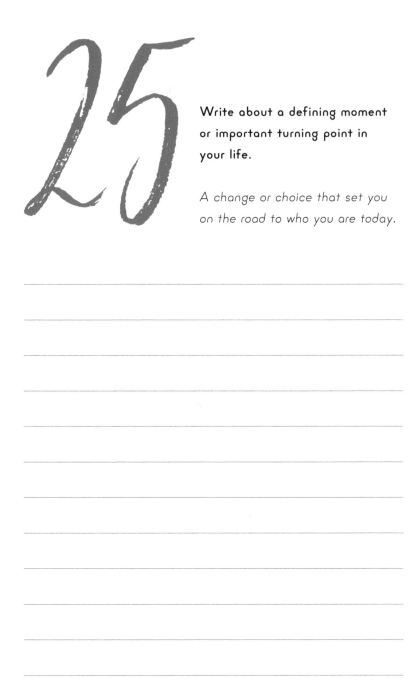

25 Write about a defining moment or important turning point in your life.

A change or choice that set you on the road to who you are today.

you choose your course

What filled you up and
energized you this week?

*Something or someone that left
you feeling more loved, excited,
encouraged or happy?*

connect with your heart & soul

What is one of your favorite childhood memories?

What makes it special? The place? The people? The feeling?

_____

_____

_____

_____

_____

_____

_____

_____

_____

_____

_____

_____

_____

find time
to look back
& smile

If you were to give this season
of your life one word, what
would it be?

*List the experiences and life lessons
that are wrapped up in this word.*

*Some
of the best
life-giving
discoveries...*

_____

_____

_____

_____

_____

_____

_____

_____

_____

_____

_____

_____

_____

_____

_____

_____

_____

_____

_____

_____

_____

_____

_____

_____

_____

_____

_____

_____

_____

_____

...are found by exploring where you've already been.

SELF
ACC
EPTA

moments of

NCE

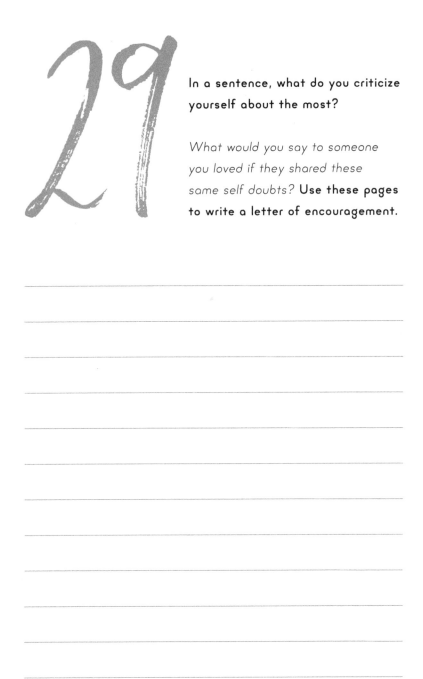

In a sentence, what do you criticize
yourself about the most?

*What would you say to someone
you loved if they shared these
same self doubts?* **Use these pages
to write a letter of encouragement.**

_____

_____

_____

_____

_____

_____

_____

_____

_____

_____

_____

Read these pages tomorrow and
the next day and the next...
until you believe it,

deep down to your core.

What would the most meaningful week of your life look like?

Who would you spend time loving? What would you want to create or accomplish? How would you want to grow and improve?

your best
will always
be enough

Look over your list and circle ONE thing to commit to doing this week. Trust that doing your best doesn't always mean doing more.

What are 5 things you love about yourself?

Pieces of your appearance, talents, characteristics...

be who you
already are

Who is someone you look up to, and what do you admire about them?

_____

_____

_____

_____

_____

_____

_____

_____

_____

_____

_____

_____

_____

let go of comparison & hold onto joy instead

Look back at the last four pages.

Both have a unique role to play.
Both hold goodness.
Both shine light.

moments of **WONDER**

Write about something you recently experienced for the first time.

A new food, a piece of furniture, a place, an accomplishment, a new skill, an adventure of the heart...

find joy
in the
undiscovered

When have you witnessed a miracle?

It could be big like a change you never imagined experiencing or a level of happiness you never imagined reaching. Or it could be small like a moment of comfort just when you needed it or a tiny reminder that you are loved.

Miracles happen...

...they really, really do.

What is one of your favorite ways
to fill your spare time?

*Describe it from the perspective
of all five senses and amplify the
joy this past time brings you -
from head to toe.*

Feel beautiful...

...because you are.

36

What inspires you?

A quote, piece of artwork, song, or someone's example?

draw courage from your inspirations

Write about how it speaks to your soul.

Maybe it brings hope during hardships, propels you to action when you'd rather just stay put, or makes that big dream feel a little more within reach.

moments of

COURAGE

**When have you ventured beyond
your comfort zone?**

*Maybe you said "yes" when you
wanted to say "no." Or chose to
head into the harder unknown
even when the safer route would
have been so much easier.*

---

live
brave

What is one of the most challenging times you've ever lived through?

Who (or what) was your source of strength?

It's through life's storms that you truly find your strength.

When have you kept going, kept trying, or kept smiling?

A time when you didn't think you had it in you, but you gave it your best anyway?

you have
more strength
than you
realize

Write about a time when a sacrifice turned out to be the best decision you ever made.

Let go of the good...

...to grab hold of the best.

moments of

INT
ENT
ION

Write about taking a step, even just a tiny one, toward a more fulfilling, happier life.

"_____ was taking me away from my happiness, and today I did something about it!"

progress
is only one
day away

In 3 words, what do you hope your life stands for?

What did you do this week to live that kind of life? How can you infuse these words into the days ahead?

live on purpose

43

What simple daily habit has brought you closer to the path you want to be on?

Sometimes all that's needed on the road to change...

Use this page to dream up your
next life-changing habit.

_...is a clear
vision of the
destination._

How would a happier version of you begin each day?

How would you greet your morning, your family, your life differently if you felt so much joy you couldn't hold it all in?

wake up with joy!

Let these pages be your guide in making
tomorrow morning your happiest morning ever!

moments
of
HO
PE

What worries or struggles
feel heavy right now?

_____

_____

_____

_____

_____

_____

_____

_____

_____

_____

_____

_____

_____

_____

Turn the page (no solutions necessary). Hold onto the hope that, despite dark cloudy skies today, there are warmer and brighter days ahead.

Always

Write down one thing you will
do differently tomorrow to make
it happier and better than today.

No guilt, only progress... and hope.

_____

_____

_____

_____

_____

_____

_____

_____

_____

_____

_____

_____

_____

within
each day lies
the possibility
of more

What about the next few weeks feels completely daunting?

there's always room for hope

Make a list of qualities, experiences,
strengths and lessons learned that
make you capable of facing this.

*(Turn back to pages 104-111 if you need to be
reminded of just how incredible you really are!)*

_____

_____

_____

_____

_____

_____

_____

_____

_____

_____

_____

48

Write about the person you hope to be one year from now.

Trust that becoming this person starts with being who you are today.

You are so very enough...

...today & always.

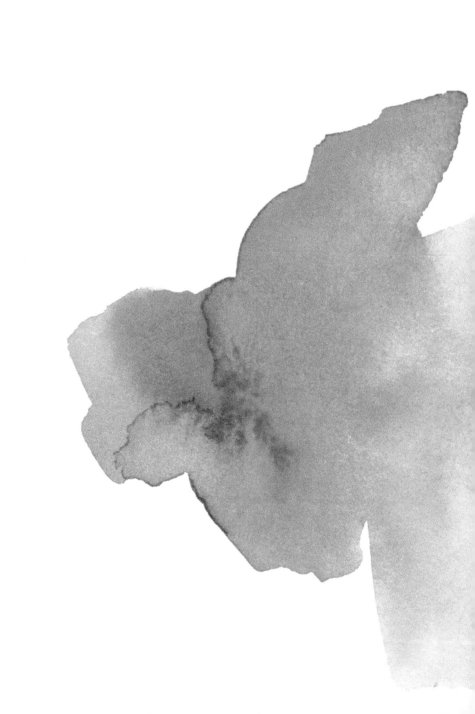

moments of TR UTH

What desires, attributes, or experiences make you different from everyone around you?

_____

_____

_____

_____

_____

_____

_____

_____

_____

_____

_____

_____

_____

live your light

You are just as unique as the part
you were destined to play. You can make
a difference BECAUSE of your differences.

What new experience, project, habit, or skill is calling to your heart?

What direction do you feel pulled to follow? What's the next step toward your truth?

_____

_____

_____

_____

_____

_____

_____

_____

_____

_____

_____

trust your truth

51

Write about a time you did something the way it felt right and true - even though it didn't follow the crowd.

Amazing things happen...

...when you
choose to head
upstream.

Make a list of things that are "so you."

Style, phrases, hobbies, foods, habits, ambitions, emotions, dreams...

_____

_____

_____

_____

_____

_____

_____

_____

_____

_____

_____

_____

_____

_____

_____

_____

This page (and all the pages before it) highlights something incredible and truly irreplaceable in this world. A brave, beautiful life full of **connection** and **creativity, intention** and **self-acceptance, reflection** and **presence**. A life that, despite everything, reflects **positivity, compassion, wonder** and **gratitude**. Found within these pages is a life that shows up with **courage, truth** and **hope**, over and over again.

Dear meaningful moment seeker, your journey is never without joy and your adventure never without purpose if you're always on the treasure hunt to find them. I hope the words - your words - now held in this book will serve as a heartfelt reminder that a life lived to the fullest is always within reach. And the moments that make it meaningful...

...are the moments that make it yours.

About the author

Anne McOmber is a writer, meaningful moment seeker and striving hope giver. With crutches in hand and two little ones underfoot, her personal stories and encouraging words inspire others to live a brave, beautiful life - even and especially when life hands us the unexpected. She shares her heart and hope at SimplicityAvenue.com, where the road to refocusing on what matters most is a bumpy but beautiful one.

You can connect with her by...

...joining her free intentional living challenge, *10 Days of Savoring the Simple Things* at **SimplicityAvenue.com**.

...or brightening her day with a note in her inbox at **anne@simplicityavenue.com**.

CPSIA information can be obtained
at www.ICGtesting.com
Printed in the USA
JSHW011352151219
2922JS00004B/114